M000194420

Kissing My Shadow

KISSING MY SHADOW

Poems

Merrill Farnsworth

SILVER BIRCH PRESS
LOS ANGELES, CALIFORNIA

© Copyright 2015, Merrill Farnsworth

Published by Silver Birch Press

ISBN-13: 978-0692403341

ISBN-10: 0692403345

FIRST EDITION: May 2015

EMAIL: silver@silverbirchpress.com

WEB: silverbirchpress.com

BLOG: silverbirchpress.wordpress.com

MAILING ADDRESS:
Silver Birch Press
P.O. Box 29458
Los Angeles, CA 90029

COVER ART: "Mardi Gras Kiss" by Merrill Farnsworth.

For Cowgirl and Buckeye
your love created poetry

TABLE OF CONTENTS

Genesis

Borders

Who drew the borders of my world?
Who decided the territories of love and hate within my
    heart?
Who built the walls in my mind to keep out dangerous
    ideas?
Who engineered dams to control the flood of my
    emotions?
Who decided the latitude and longitude of my soul?
Who set limits on the heights to which my spirit can soar?
Your voice is stuck in my head.
My face is trapped in the mirror.
One shattering move and I slip through fissured glass
beyond the borders of my reflection
charting a new course.
I will love what I love and hate what I hate.
I will kiss the Grand Inquisitor on the lips.
I will dash into the flames with every woman set on fire.
I will whirl like a dervish toward the sun
then tumble from the sky with singed wings
falling into the one true story of my life.

Textures and Hues

I did not choose the texture and hues
or build the loom
I simply entered the world.
Fate chose the fabric
spun from tumbleweeds and tornadoes,
carbon black creeping under windowsills
burnt orange flames licking the sky
like tongues of thirsty dragons
reaching from the belly of the oil refinery
where my father staked his claim
on a bright future at age twenty-two
with his chemical engineering degree,
and his new wife, both hearts brimming
with post war optimism.
My young mother gifted me
with hues of sun-bleached cow skulls,
dirt brown horned toads,
amber fire ants and soft gray tones
of mockingbird feathers gathered from the land
where she learned to rope wayward calves
and pin squealing bodies tight to the ground
as the red hot shape of the family brand
burned deep into their hides.
My tapestry began spinning
one harsh December morning
near Amarillo where I would see
the bright yellow yolk of an egg
frying on the sidewalk in summer,
the halcyon blue of translucent icicles
hanging from cottonwoods in winter,
the gathering storm in my mother's eyes,
the flashing sunshine in my father's smile
as he walked through the door
somewhere past five to rescue us all:
my mother with a kiss and a cocktail,
me with a playful toss in the air,
my sister with a nuzzle to neck,
my unborn brother with an open hand
spread full on my mother's belly,
my soon to be conceived brother
with a twinkle in his eyes,
himself with a hope the American Dream
would out-spin the six o'clock news.

Wild Pony

Thank you for your fierce gaze
watching me eat my corn flakes,
making me restless for freedom.
The screen door slams behind me
as I dash on skinny legs,
my hair a sun-spiked halo
a peanut butter sandwich in my pocket.
I shimmy under the barbed wire fence
to a field where the wild cherry grows.
Tall grass tickles my shins. Mayflies rise.
I climb fearless to the highest branch
riding the wild pony of the wind.

Soul Food

Such a mess. You.
Sticky as Mississippi mud.
The beginnings
of a flourless chocolate cake.
Then Ivory soap. A petticoat.
Sitting pretty in Sunday school.
Iced white like a wedding cake.
The preacher says pray.
Pray that God
will save your soul.
You pray. Neither you
or the preacher
grasping the untame
nature of a soul.
I'm here
just under your skin
waiting for the snap
of your psyche. The crack
in your defenses. The rip
of the mask. The release.
One drop of eternity
clinging to the fleshy pink
rim of your lip. Taste
the rich, dark
bittersweet flavor
of answered prayer.

Map of the World

It is August. Late summer light
streams through the window
as cicadas begin to hum.
I sit at the green Formica table
in the corner of your kitchen
studying a map of the world,
the same map pinned to the wall
when my father was a child.
You open the cellar door
to fetch potatoes from
the dusky earth below.
Cool. Musty. Old.
I stare at distant coastlines
and dangling peninsulas
as you take chicken and butter
from the humming Frigidaire
dredging breasts and thighs
in golden yokes and snow white flour
to work a woman's alchemy
of fire, pink flesh and extra crispy.
Beneath shapes of oceans and continents
I place rose pattern plates on the table
where we sit and eat, breathing in and out,
this moment our dot on the map of the world.

She'll Be Fine

One
Saturday morning.
Whirling blades on burnt grass,
fire ants scatter as rattlers slide.
Then a bunny. The mower halts.
A father's gentle hands reach
to rescue fragile life.
This won't end well
says the mother.
A rancher's daughter knows
nature's rough ways.

Two
Sunday morning.
The predicted bunny funeral
in the backyard.
Three children stare
as their sister keens.
She'll be fine,
says the mother.
A soft broken shape
curls like a curio
inside a girl's heart.

Three
Saturday morning.
She is fine.
A fat golden puppy
sturdy enough for love
squirms, licks and wriggles
inside her adamant embrace.

Tumbling Towards the Sky

Horse hooves hammering
hard on salt packed sand
silver tipped sea foam
dancing wild at dawn
wind through my hair
sun rising fast
fully alive
before I knew the fear of falling.
Through the rabbit hole
horse and rider go
stirring up a tempest in a teacup
galloping round and round
towards an impossible horizon
fissuring the delicate bone china
splattering tea leaves in dark patterns
as the teacup tips over spilling me head first
into my grandmother's garden
planted carefully with morning glories
trumpet vines, tiger lilies and sage
the garden where I climbed the beanstalk
artfully escaping the giant's grasp
tumbling towards the sky.

Coming of Age in Guayama

I turn 13 in Guayama
City of the Witches
where black madonnas speak
ancient mysteries spiced deep
with pungent truth and dark beauty
while nuns count rosary beads
praying earnest and low at the altar.
Sidewalk vendors brown and lean
sell slices of juicy ripe mango flesh
while packs of restless young men
pass a bottle of Bacardi
guzzling courage and howling
as sultry beauties lull along in twos
rolling full hips and flirtatious eyes
while I stumble by, blond hair
scattered like straw in the sunlight,
embarrassed when they hiss *Americana.*
I turn 13 among sugar cane fields,
wind-swept shanties, blood sausage,
pigeon peas, rice and roasted plantains,
my body absorbing the gallops
of a speckled horse wild and fearless
racing across miles of bleached sand
kissing boys who know each step
of the samba on a Saturday night.
I turn 13 on an island of full moon tides
where fortunetellers peer into midnight
and stoic priests absolve every sin.
I stand outside the cathedral walls
craving the taste of confession.

Love Chapter

Wide-eyed and 16 I listen to you
rhapsodize about perfect love.
The dazzle of you on me
inspires immediate eviction
of each flaw threatening my debut
as your bright angel.
I outlaw impatience. I order selfish
desire to wander the desert alone.
I try starving pride to become small.
Anger is banished by a blind belief
you mean no wrong. Despair is voted out.
Skepticism is shunned. Doubt is sent packing.
Failure is not allowed. For years
I hover above thoughts of leaving.
I crush restlessness at the border.
I order drone strikes on rogue emotions.
What I fail to imagine
are the refugees of my true nature
rising to fight like mad for their homeland.
They drag me down, cut my wings,
put me on trial, expose my humanity,
forgive me, and demand starring roles
in the next chapter of my life.

Weight of Love

The weight of love
is a flood drowning her
before she blossoms.
The weight of love
is light bearing down
just as he opens his eyes.
The weight of love
is a kiss silencing her
as she parts lips to speak.
Let love be weightless
as cottonwood
gone to seed.

Beware the Woo Woo

You need to be careful, she said,
not to get carried away with
animal images in your writing.
Snakes, bears and the like
make you sound like a cliché —
like one of those women
who (look of disdain)
"runs with the wolves."

I am what I am:
a native Texan who learned moxie
from three rattlers sunning on a rock,
a young girl living in Puerto Rico
caught up in the palm tree's sway,
a 16 year old who gave her heart
to a shape-shifter in South Carolina,
a troubled young woman in Tennessee
visited by hummingbirds and transformed
from trembling rabbit to fierce mother bear.

Did I mention I'm from a long line
of practical, hard working people
valuing rational views and common sense?
These logical voices are always in my head
but if a wolf invites me to run I will say yes.

Essence

Time and pressure distill me
into the essence of this journey:
scent of sky, earth, jasmine, sandalwood,
cedar and tumbleweeds on a Texas plain.
Drop of moon glow, fleck from the crest
of a tsunami racing towards an unassuming shore.
Just enough poison to serve as an antidote
for the world and its ways.
Local honey, shot of whiskey, vinegar,
sass and sympathy for the Devil.
Stretch of a cat, wail of the wind, dandelion seeds
carrying scattered wishes to the neighbor's yard.
Blackberries ripening in the summer sun,
fog rolling across cliffs of ancient pine,
defiance laced with delta blues.
Whispers from a lost horizon.
Dusk soaked laughter. Skeptic's gaze.
A seeker's endless journey.
Restless wings. Tangled embrace.
Mercurial moods. Magnolia in May.

Rock a Bye

I want to live
on the edge of a cliff
near the wild blue sea
but I am afraid.

Rock a bye, rock a bye

I open the door
a tiger springs forth
I will eat you up, he says.
Please don't, I say.

Rock a bye, rock a bye.

Alright, says the tiger,
his eyes flashing topaz
in the darkening light,
follow me in the storm,
hold your head high,
growl at the wind.

Rock a bye, rock a bye

I dance in the tiger's
terrible stripes
on the edge of a cliff
in the wild blue sea.

Rock a bye, rock a bye

Pilgrims & Prodigals

Maybe Rapture

She wears life on her face like a tattoo.
He's pierced from head to toe. Renegade
souls at the bus stop of 4th and Main
clutching tickets to Armageddon.

She's looks him up and down
counting each perilous memory pierced
 into his brow, his ears, his lips.
She imagines he can kill. Maybe her.

Sneaking a glance he finds flint grey eyes
daring him to study each line of her face
etched with the ink of reckless courage.
He imagines she can survive. Maybe him.

When the bus rolls around at midnight
 they sit side by side in flickering light.
Her fingers trace his lips. His eyes adore her face.
They imagine a confederacy of two. Maybe rapture.

Pilgrims of My Longing

Today I will not want.
I will not regret.
I will not strive.
Today will be enough.
I will not dream
or remember yesterday.
I will not wonder, or worry, or resolve.
My soul will not dig deeper.
My spirit will not fly higher.
My heart will not wander or seek safe harbor.
If the storm rages I will give myself to the wind.
If a seed takes root I will let it bloom.
If the day is done I will let go.
Today my vagabond stands still
content to gaze at the stars until dawn
when the pilgrims of my longing return.

.

Lake Michigan

They are out of their element
staring through plate glass windows
into cold Chicago winter.
He sees her in new light
and feeling a chill
she walks past him
to find the cherry wood box
given in the heat of love.
Dropping her gold ring
inside for safe keeping
she fails to see their vows
vanish beneath Lake Michigan.

Holy Fire

It seemed a worthy trade,
my soul for a leading role
in a beautiful dream
fed daily with sacrifices
of living truth.
Now the Devil or
maybe God breathes
into me with fire so hot
it burns down the world.
My next breath
is a brand new day.

Bible Belt Boy

Black. Raven curls
tendriled soft and sweet
as his mother holds him close
praying his heart will never break
when God knows her prayer
is that he won't break hers.
Black. The Holy Bible
delivered page by page
by a father to save a son's soul
unaware he is hoping
his son will save his.
Grey. The gun
his grandfather keeps in a drawer
gambling he'll shoot an intruder
when the true gamble
is not to kill one of his own.
Yellow. The pills
his father's brother swallows
to silence demons
when sympathy for the Devil
could have softened their screams.
Blue. Mud soaked notes clinging
hard to the soles of his feet
when he tries to wash them clean
heading west across the Mississippi.
White. Pages flying free from rigid bindings
as he scales peaks far from Southern heat.
Red. The passion of the climb,
live or die, to find home.

Bridge View Inn

We speed toward the Pacific
on four wheels toward a break down.
I don't see it in the manic flicker
of the vacancy sign at the Bridgeview Inn.
Perhaps I sense it in the sharp edge
of the innkeeper's tone as she scans my license.
Trail of Tears, she says. *That's bad land.*
Actually, I say, *we're on our way to the Badlands.*
She points at a portrait of Lewis and Clark.
Meriwether Lewis didn't die in South Dakota.
It's Tennessee that took him under. I tell her
he was complicated. *Land can't rise up to take*
a person down. She scowls into her cheekbones
handing me the key to a river front room.
It sinks undetected into my bones as we sit
side by side on the banks of the Missouri
drinking Fish Eye and eating avocado sandwiches.
Two glasses deep into the bottle, Meriwether's ghost
floats by on a raft. I catch him calling you
with his knowing, brilliant, beautiful gaze. *I've got this*,
you say, scuttling down snake-infested river rocks
to dip your toes in the wake of his journey, your journey
to discover new territory and fight old demons.
Eve! I shout. D*on't go.* You laugh, undaunted, knowing
one bite of an apple a serpent offered you long ago
still carries courage to survive anything. Even Tennessee.

Wheels on the Bus

Ricci,ticci,tac,click,clack
chug, yearn, reach
the green-eyed girl
rides a rickety bus
careening toward Nirvana.
Ricci,ticci,tac,click,clack
chug, yearn, reach
the bus driver winks
a turquoise dragon roars
the dharma wheel spins.
Ricci,ticci,tac,click,clack
chug, yearn, reach
the green eyed girl
trusts this journey
more than life
Ricci,ticci,tac,click,clack
chug, yearn, reach
her hope coils tight
as the unborn sky
waiting to unfurl.
Ricci,ticci,tac,click,clack
chug, yearn, reach
the wheels on the bus
spin round and round.

She's Pretty

She was abandoned.
Down and out in South Carolina.
Afraid of thunder. Half starved.
Yowling in the storm.
Tender hearted he fed her,
put her in the car and drove
all the way home to Tennessee.
Mama and sisters approved.
The house had two gingers.
She made three. The other two
didn't last the year. Whether
it was she that did them in
or she that saved the house
from lack of a ginger tabby —
this will never be known.
Everyone wants to touch her.
She's pretty, they say, reaching
to pet her soft, luxurious body.
Sometimes she accepts.
Sometimes she bites.
It's clear she's wild they say
she's not to be trusted.
We trust her to be what she is:
a cat rescued from a storm
last summer in South Carolina.

Cowgirl and Buckeye

Give me the odds of a dare devil from Ohio
and a rancher's daughter from Texas colliding
over chemistry in New Mexico.
Go West, young man his mother said
sending her only son far away
from the family tree. She didn't
see him slip a buckeye in his pocket
to bring him luck. His luck was 19,
all five feet and one inch of her
laying down the law of love.
No crying over spilled milk she said
and no breaking things. Like vows.
He winked and married her
wanting nothing more than her
brand of a sure thing.
Their first child was a prodigal,
the second so pretty, the third so kind,
the fourth climbed determined
toward the sun. All four
face East Texas and on any given day
imagine the Cowgirl and the Buckeye
watching wild geese rise raucous
honking praise for two everyday magicians
who turned spilled milk into a sky full of stars.

Most Days

When she's in the mood for solitude
she can make a cat feel lonely and a dog,
if she had one, well, he might as well go next door
for the fond pat on the head he deserves.
But stick around and she'll fry up
extra helpings of sunshine for breakfast
heaping huge servings of joy on your plate
as hummingbirds hover above her head.
At night she wraps herself around you;
arms, legs and elbows twined
in a tangle of ivy, evergreen and ash.
You wake to find her burrowing
into your arms like a soft animal.
You stroke her hair, pull her close
wondering when the wilds of Wyoming
will call her to wander hollow canyons.
You know you love her. Most days.

Storm Season

Hot meets cold
twisting the sky inside out
driving toward Memphis
it's midnight in mid afternoon.
Fields on fire with lighting strikes.
Hail clattering on the windshield.
In a minute the rain comes
pouring down like Noah's flood
and we, like all the other sinners,
race toward shelter, hearts beating fast,
wedged between a pair of big rigs
hovering above us like giant bugs.
The sky turns sick shades of sulfur.
Black clouds take shape like wraiths.
Air clashes. Cyclones spin.
A Wonder Bread sign flies by
and we laugh. You and me
rocked by the wind. Nowhere to go.
Nothing to do but wait it out
in this landscape of delta blues.

A Game of Gin

Yes. I'll stare at the moon.
That's what I do. Join me.
Hold my hand. We'll gaze
deep into melancholy's pool
the heat between us
softening old scars.
Then can we go inside?
I'll fetch the snacks
lots and lots of them
the kind that make us fat
and keep us warm
while you deal the cards.
We'll play for Italy and Spain
eventually dividing the world
between us. Then let's light a fire
and have fun whether or not
the world is laughing with us.
Let's take the lids off
all the boxes and jump out.
At dawn we'll open the windows
and let song birds fly in
to perch on our heads.
I'll make toast
scattering crumbs of our joy
across the living room as music
we couldn't hear a moment ago rises
so irresistibly we forget life is sad.
Let's use up all the sunshine in one day.
When winter comes early
due to our excess, we'll huddle up
and deal out the cards
for another game of gin.
One of us will win Tahiti.
If it's me, I'll share.

Nashville 159

Early one October morning I leave,
crossing the Cumberland Plateau,
climbing steady toward the Great Smokies
trading Tennessee for North Carolina
where narrow lanes of asphalt find me
snaking down steep run-away curves
sandwiched between a truck and a rock wall
holding my breath speeding past all 18 wheels
barely making it around the hazardous bend
when the world opens revealing fiery ridges
blazing fierce beneath a dusting of snow.
These mountains echo the landscape of my heart
pulsing with fire and ice.
Returning to you the night sky illuminates the sign
Nashville 159. I'm flooded with all that we are.
One headlight leads me all the way home.

My Judas

Let me rock you all night long
in the garden of thistles and thorns
where wild roses bloom.
Let me love you
back to the bend in the road
where you stared into a sky
sprawled with spiraling stars,
each light a simple wish
for warmth on a cold night.
Let me untangle the roots
twisting daylight to darkness
making a palm itch
for thirty pieces of silver.
Let me kiss your lips
before they betray
the one you love.

Forgiveness

I sit on the bridge between two worlds
under the shadow of an Appalachian pine,
branches reaching toward Carolina blue sky.
I feel the restless rise of the unspoken
fluttering in my chest like the untested wings
of a caged bird. *No*, I say, *not yet.*

Maybe tomorrow I will hear the cry
of the wild bird within as she escapes my grasp,
spreading her wings in effortless flight
as the stone rolls away and my heart flies free.

Summer Heat

My hair is on fire
my engine is blown
even the sprinkler
is spurting out flames

It's so damn hot
the chicken is frying itself
my entire house is an Easy Bake Oven
and the cat is dancing on a hot tin roof

It's so damn hot
all my defenses are melting
my No Trespassing signs have gone fishing
my storm door is flung open wide

Cross the threshold fool
run heedless into this house on fire
ignore the alarm and kiss me
even our bones will burn

Poem (sirens, penny, pirates)

1.

In a dark room sirens wail

we share space between hope and horror

holding tight to the absence of light

shadows write poems on the wall

2.

a walk in the park

a shiny penny

two hands reach

heads or tails

you smile

pressing this moment

into my palm

3.

shipwrecked on different islands

we chart a course toward common ground

not even sharks or pirates can stop us

just like that we cross the ocean between us

Revelations

Waking the Wolf

Thrust into this world without warning
I am waiting to catch first breath
when the tiger has no claws
and all bloodlust is forgotten.
I am waiting to break my vow
not to breathe until the war is won
the city is rebuilt and love never dies.
I am waiting for Humpty Dumpty
to get it together again after falling.
Shattered by the clarity of imperfection
I gulp the air of anguish and wonder
unleashing an exquisite newborn howl
that wakes the wolf at the door
the witch in the woods
and the mirror on the wall.

Inspired by Lawrence Ferlinghetti's poem "I Am Waiting"
and first published by Silver Birch Press in the
I AM WAITING Poetry Series (December 2014).

Kissing My Shadow

I saw you skipping untethered
before I knew the word *doppelgänger,*
before I knew to fill you flush
with secrets unfit for mama,
polite company or me. I thrive
casting false light until the day you
heave upward: Christ from the tomb.
Now you walk slow by my side
dark and solemn at high noon leading
me inside a stone labyrinth.
The sign at the entrance says forgive.
My hate feels holy
but you feel no need for revenge
so urge me to sacred ground.
Round and round we travel deep
into the circle within the circle.
Then in front of God and everyone
you bring me to my knees
and I kiss you full on the lips
every secret tasting like forgiveness.

New Hallelujah

Damn. Chicken Little was right.
The sky fell. All the stars too.
Good. It's over. I can officially
quit trying to hold up a world
created with plucky courage,
misplaced hope and worn out clichés.
I will nestle down inside out
folding, collapsing, closing my eyes
in surrender to the sweet ether of unbelief.
Floating somewhere between God and the Devil
I find the North Star shining just below my skin
a pulsing diamond tattooed on every cell,
a reckless joy singing
a new hallelujah under a weightless sky.

Strange Brew

I wake up craving any life not my own
when a face takes shape within a feathered snap.
Wings. Razor cut. Tipped with red dirt.
Maybe blood. Mine.
Time to reap what you've sown
says a voice thick with bramble and vine. I rise
clutching a blade in one hand and a torch in the other
facing fields I refuse to claim. Fields scattered with:
lies told to keep promises,
fear more fantastic than pride,
ideas that seemed good at the time.
I toss forth the torch to burn every field
but a mad flutter of wings extinguishes the flame.
A blade is the proper tool for the harvest. Let me help.
His odd tone of merriment makes me curious.
Side by side we reap fields rippled with fear and lies,
fields strewn with honest kisses, skin against skin,
fields rich with moments I was strong enough
to caress the barbed edges of another
stirring up love and hate
mulling, stewing, distilling a strange brew.
The trickster angel cups his hands like chalice
into all that I am, laughing long and loud
as I savor the complex hues of my life.

Confession

How they love life, my seven or so
Deadly Sins reveling in redemption.
How they rejoice, bouncing and begging
not to be cast aside like embarrassing children.
Look! Says Sloth. I'm up here dancing with Lust.
Blushing at the intensity of their liturgical writhing
I kneel and close my eyes, joining other voices
begging for mercy already given.
Greed finds an unexpected 20 in my wallet,
places it in the collection plate and waves at Gluttony
who stands at the altar serving communion.
I sweat it out hoping she doesn't cram the
wafers in her own mouth like French fries.
Pride pats me in the shoulder. *Relax,* she says.
Meanwhile Envy stares hard at Christ
calling to her from inside the Tiffany window
as the stained glass melts into sky.
In one motion my seven sisters and I rise,
running toward Emmaus. Confessing joy.

Born Again

It is winter.
You can let go.
If disappointment
has taken root
let it die.
If a cup of cold misery
is your morning beverage
pour it down the drain
and make hot chocolate.
If darkness is blooming inside
like a hot house flower
send it outside to build a snowman.
If life is old and dull
bury it in the garden
where it can rise
in brilliant shades of red.
It is winter.
It is the dying time.
You can let go
and be born again.

Melting Blue Ice

Dark and empty, God forsaken,
cold as the desert at night.
Remote as the dark side of the moon,
hard as stone, hollow as a black hole:
this ancient place in my heart
where blue ice dwells.
Too blue to say yes,
holding tight to treasured pain,
playing tricks on my better self.
Whispering resentments and jealousies,
cagey and defensive, saying no to mystery,
to redemption, to love, to life.
This sapphire blazing,
this frozen memory
in the middle of my heart
surrounded by tender flesh.
Soft flesh that says yes.
Living flesh that says feel.
Trembling flesh that says
imagine a honey-hued dawn
embracing indigo night.
Feel the warmth
of Passion's light
melting blue ice.

Gabriel's Wings

Sometimes melancholy paints my mind gunmetal gray.
Like Persephone I'm pulled into shadow,
the tiger lily's shape a lost embrace, just out of reach.
Then deep within the tone of hollow days,
Gabriel's wings unfurl, slicing emptiness into ribbons of
    light.

Encounter with a Fiery Oak

Breathe! She shouts to me
as I walk beneath her canopy
of crimson leaves.
Why do you hold so greedy
to one shallow breath
refusing to let go?
I know that once upon a time
life taught you to play dead -
a useful survival instinct
for possums, rabbits
and frightened children.
Look! It worked.
Here you stand, half alive.
Breathe! She urges.
Take a belly breath.
Inhale the poison with the pure.
Now exhale, empty out,
burn down the world
with dragon fire
as I take mercurial toxins
of lingering memory and fear
into my tangled roots
reaching for quickening streams
of living water to baptize
every demon's breath.
Do not be afraid!
You are not a small-voiced child,
a slinking possum,
or a rabbit caught in a hunter's snare.
You are a woman.
Breathe, she whispers,
a low branch brushing
tender across my cheek
as I breathe autumn's fiery light.

Emmaus Rising

You look at me
I do not see your face.
You speak to me
I do not hear your voice.
You touch me
I feel nothing.
All the while
my head is spinning,
my heart is pounding,
my soul is aching
with countless desires.
Then, breathing deeply,
I come to that moment
when time stands still.
I give up my yearnings,
I quiet my questions,
I quit looking
for what I think
I should see . . .
I see you.

Dream Work

Somewhere between waking and dreaming
there is a yawn then a twilight haze
then a breeze through the tall grass that is God

Somewhere between waking and dreaming
there is a yearning then the laughter
then an ache when you are gone

Somewhere between waking and dreaming
there is the tightrope then the terror
then a lightening flash of the perfect scheme

Somewhere between waking and dreaming
There is the illusion then the lust
then the sharp edge of bone against bone

Somewhere between waking and dreaming
there is a melting then love's unexpected shape
then the wanting of all that I have

Living Crazy Brave

It's not about holding back the tears when life hurts
it's about surfing the tsunami of grief and maybe
    drowning.

It's not about fighting off the love that will break your
    heart
it's about being cracked wide open and sucked inside out.

It's not about being as fierce or wild as a tiger
it's about dancing in the tiger's terrible stripes.

It's not about being strong or destined for glory
it's about clinging to the fragile threads of dignity.

It's not about planting both feet on the snow peaked
    summit
it's about the vertigo of failure plunging you deep into
    grace.

It's not about pulling up by bootstraps or soldiering on as
    arrows fly
it's standing naked as love unravels every tangled scheme of
    survival.

ABOUT THE AUTHOR

A Texas tumbleweed, Merrill Farnsworth came of age immersed in the sights and sounds of Puerto Rico's Afro-Caribbean culture. The cadences of South Carolina left their mark on her, as well as melodies reaching from Appalachia to the Mississippi Delta. Just like most everyone in Nashville, Merrill writes songs, including ASCAP award winner *Heaven's Heart*. Recent cuts (with Phil Madeira) by Dan Tyminski, The McCrary Sisters, and Jason Eskridge can be found on itunes and Amazon (*Mercyland: Hymns for the Rest of Us*).

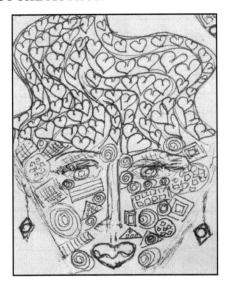

**Drawing from poetry journal
by Merrill Farnsworth**

60708522R00035

Made in the USA
Charleston, SC
04 September 2016